The Colourful West Country

Descriptive text by A.N. Court

The Colourful West Country

Jarrold Colour Publications, Norwich

Bath Abbey rises majestically above the remarkable Roman Baths (1).
L'Abbaye de Bath s'élève au-dessus des Bains Romains (1).
Die Abtei von Bath erhebt sich über den römischen Bädern (1).

Somerset

Somerset – 'smiling Somerset' – famous for its cheeses and its cider, is the gateway to the West. The name of the county is derived from that of a Saxon tribe, but long before their coming the region was inhabited by Celts who have left traces of their occupation in a few place names. There are links, too, with the Arthurian legends, and King Arthur himself is said to have been buried at Glastonbury. The Roman occupation of Somerset is abundantly evident in Bath and along the roads that they constructed across the country, the most important of which forms part of the Fosse Way and runs through the county from Chard to Bath. In 1685 the last battle to be fought on English soil took place in Somerset, when the Duke of Monmouth's abortive rebellion came to an end at the Battle of Sedgemoor. Somerset men paid dearly for their support of the Duke, and scores of them were sentenced by the infamous Judge Jeffries to be hanged for their complicity in the rebellion. Geographically the county is somewhat complex, but it may for convenience be divided into three main areas, each of which has its own particular character. Northern Somerset belongs to Bath, to Wells and to Cheddar; it is a region of history and of prehistory, whose origins are as old as the Mendip Hills which contain the majestic cliffs of Cheddar and the mysterious depths of Wookey Hole. To the west of the River Parrett lies quite another region, with the county town of Taunton as its outpost. Here are the Quantock and Brendon Hills and beyond them the lonely slopes of Exmoor. And where these green hills sweep down to the sea lie some of the loveliest of villages and townships – Selworthy, Watchet, Porlock and Minehead, whose Church Steps rival Clovelly's famous High Street for quaint beauty. The traveller who explores further to the south will find much to reward him, charming towns, fine old mansions, and everywhere the glorious countryside of Somerset, a county rich in legend, in history and in associations. At every turn there is something to be admired and something to be remembered.

2

The Bristol Avon has a total length of about seventy-five miles and in its lower reaches flows in an impressive gorge, spanned by the famous Clifton Suspension Bridge (2) which links Bristol with the beautiful Somerset countryside. The bridge was first planned as long ago as 1753, but it was more than a hundred years before the project was finally completed. Bath, the only true eighteenth-century city in England, is justly famous for the splendour of its Georgian architecture, for its stately Abbey Church and for its truly remarkable Roman Baths. The Abbey Church is the successor to a great Norman building, of which only fragments remain. Of the second church, built at the end of the fifteenth century, only the West Front (3) survives, for after the Reformation the church fell into decay and was not rebuilt until the beginning of the seventeenth century. For more than 1900 years the spa waters of Bath have been sought for their curative properties; the Romans valued the waters and built a considerable establishment, which has been intelligently excavated and reconstructed. In the eighteenth century Richard 'Beau' Nash transformed Bath into the most fashionable social milieu in England, and it was in this period that Robert Adam built Pultney Bridge (4), which spans the Avon and is one of the few remaining bridges in England with shops along both sides. If you climb to Poets Walk on the top of the green cliffs, from where Turner loved to paint his sunsets, you look down towards Clevedon (5), a charming seaside town and a good centre for exploring the Gordano countryside.

Bristol, capitale commerciale de l'Ouest, est une ville importante au bord de la rivière Avon. La rivière passe par un défilé imposant (Avon Gorge) enjambé par le célèbre Clifton Suspension Bridge (2). La façade ouest de l'Abbatiale de Bath (3) date du 15e siècle, mais le reste du bâtiment fut érigé deux siècles plus tard. Au 18e siècle Bath devint le milieu social le plus élégant de l'Angleterre. Pultney Bridge (4) enjambe la rivière Avon. Clevedon (5) est une charmante station balnéaire à la côte nord du Somerset. Du sommet des falaises Turner peignit le coucher du soleil.

Die Clifton Suspension Bridge (Aufhängebrücke) überspannt den Bristol Avon und verbindet Bristol mit der Grafschaft Somerset. Bath ist gleichermaßen bekannt für die vielen Häuser im georgischen Stil, seine prächtige Abteikirche und die römischen Bäder. Die Westfront der Abteikirche (3) stammt aus dem 15. Jahrhundert, aber der größere Teil ist jünger. Im 18. Jh. wurde Bath zum elegantesten Treffpunkt Englands. Die Pultney brücke (4) über den Avon ist eine der wenigen Brücken mit Läden auf beiden Seiten. Clevedon (5) ist ein reizender Badeort an der Nordküste von Somerset.

4

5

6

7

8

Brockley Combe (6), au nord-est de Cleeve, sur la route Bristol – Weston-super-Mare, a de ravissants pentes boisées. Weston-super-Mare est un centre de villégiature très populaire sur la côte de Somerset avec terrains de golf, tennis et charmant jardin (7). A Weston, la plage sablonneuse (8) attire nombre de jeunes mais est concurrencée par la piscine d'eau de mer de South Beach. Célèbre défilé du Cheddar (9) dont les grottes ont été habitées par « l'Homme du Cheddar » il y a 80 000 ans.

Brockley Combe (6) ist eine schöne Bergschlucht nordöstlich von Cleeve. Weston-super-Mare ist eines der beliebtesten Ferienorte Somersets, Hauptanziehungspunkt für Hunderte von Urlaubern sind der Ziergarten (7) hinter dem Wintergartenpavillion und der Sandstrand (8). Die berühmte Schlucht von Cheddar (9) ist eine der Naturwunder Englands. Die Axe bildete diese Höhlen, die in prähistorischer Zeit bewohnt waren.

Brockley Combe (6) is a delightful glen which is entered from the main road between Bristol and Weston-super-Mare, a short distance north-east of Cleeve. The combe runs inland between well-wooded hillsides towards Chew Magna. The combe takes its name from the village of Brockley where St Nicholas' Church stands within the grounds of Brockley Court, the home of the Pigott family. Considerable restoration of the church was undertaken by the Pigotts between 1820 and 1830. A century ago Weston-super-Mare was a tiny fishing village; today it is one of the most popular holiday towns on the Somerset coast, attracting many visitors who find here all the amenities of a first-class resort. At the rear of the Winter Gardens Pavilion are tennis courts, putting greens and an attractive formal garden (7). Weston has two piers: the older joins the mainland to the tiny island of Birnbeck, and it is from here that pleasure steamers sail for Cardiff, Bristol and Ilfracombe. The more modern Grand Pier is nearly half a mile long and has an elaborate pavilion. The sandy beach (8) is the main attraction for thousands of youngsters, but it has a powerful rival in the huge sea-water bathing pool on the South Beach. On the wooded slopes behind the town and within sight of the esplanade is Worlebury Camp, an Iron Age relic of considerable antiquarian interest. Almost a hundred circular pits have been found, which appear to have been used as storage places for food. Human remains have also been discovered, some of them bearing signs of having met a violent end. Two islands, Flat Holme and Steep Holme, lie off Weston, and on most days the Welsh coastline is visible across the wide Severn Estuary. Cheddar's famous gorge (9) is one of the wonders of England. The best way to view it is to descend the road which winds along the bottom of the gorge between perpendicular cliffs which in places tower 400 feet above the roadway. Geologists tell us that the gorge was once the course of an underground river and that at some time the roof caved in. The River Axe is indeed underground here and the waters have formed the celebrated caves of Cheddar, which were known in the twelfth century and rediscovered in the nineteenth. That the caves were inhabited in prehistoric times is an established fact, for many bone implements have been discovered as well as the remains of the 'Cheddar Man', variously estimated to be between 40,000 and 80,000 years old. In the upper part of the gorge the cliffs are less precipitous and their outline is softened by vegetation.

The little village of Woolverton lies right in the east of Somerset near the Wiltshire border. Like many of the hostelries of these parts the Red Lion Inn (10) is an extremely attractive building and boasts an outside stairway leading to the upper floor. There are sundials incised into the walls of the church and some good carving in the interior. Another and older inn is the George (11) at Norton St Philips, a little way to the north-west. The George dates from the fifteenth century and is one of the earliest examples of its type. Here again there are outside stairs to an upper room. The inn numbers several notabilities among its visitors: Samuel Pepys and Oliver Cromwell both stayed here and it is said that the Duke of Monmouth was a resident just before the Battle of Sedgemoor and that he narrowly escaped a would-be assassin's bullet fired through the window. The most interesting feature of the church here, of approximately the same date as the inn, is its west tower, which is a curious mixture of architectural styles. For twelve centuries there has been a church at Wells. The present cathedral and the incomparable group of buildings which surround it are unique. They stand today as a living example of the pattern of an ecclesiastical city as it was when the church was the supreme authority. A wonderful collection of carved figures, some of them larger than life size, adorn the magnificent West Front (12), which is one of the architectural glories of England. The Early English central tower is supported inside the cathedral by curious architectural figures of eight, or inverted arches, which were inserted early in the fourteenth century. Some of the finest medieval glass in England is to be seen in the east window, above the High Altar. The cathedral possesses an intricate mechanical clock, originally made by a monk of Glastonbury in the fourteenth century. Every quarter of an hour a figure known as 'Jack Blandiver' kicks a bell with his heels. For more than a century the swans on the pool of the Bishop's Palace have been accustomed to give audible notice of their need for food; they pull on a rope attached to a bell.

A Woolverton, « the Red Lion Inn » (10) est d'un attrait irrésistible. A Norton St Philips se trouve une autre auberge, plus ancienne, du 15ᵉ siècle, « the George » (11), où séjournèrent Samuel Pepys, et Oliver Cromwell aussi bien que (cathédrale) le duc de Monmouth avant la bataille de Sedgemoor. Le clocher ouest de l'église est un curieux mélange de style. Quant à Wells, sa cathédrale est unique, avec sa magnifique collection de statues sculptées sur la façade ouest (12), et son horloge mécanique du 14ᵉ siècle avec un personnage « Jack Blandiver » qui heurte une cloche du pied chaque quart d'heure. Sur l'étang du Bishop's Palace, les cygnes, eux aussi, sonnent une cloche, quand ils veulent leur nourriture.

Das kleine Dorf Woolverton liegt nahe der Grenze zu Wiltshire und wie viele Wirtshäuser in diesem Gebiet ist der Red Lion (10) ein ausgesprochen schönes Gebäude. Das Gasthaus the George (11) in Norton St Philip ist über 400 Jahre alt. Viele bekannte Persönlichkeiten waren hier zu Gast. Seit zwölf Jahrhunderten steht eine Kirche in Wells. Ein wunderbares Beispiel einer Kirchenstadt finden wir in der heutigen Kathedrale mit den sie umgebundenen Gebäuden. Die Westfassade der Kathedrale (12) wird von überlebensgroßen Figuren geschmückt. Der zentrale Turm wird im Innern von Bogen getragen, die im 14. Jh. eingefügt wurden. Über dem Hochaltar befindet sich ein schönes mittelalterliches Glasfenster.

13

Nunney Castle (13) is in the east of Somerset between Shepton Mallet and Frome. It was built by Sir John Delamere in 1373 and was modelled on the Bastille in Paris. During the Civil War it was besieged and the ruins are now preserved as an Ancient Monument. Glastonbury may well be called the cradle of Christianity in England, for it is so old that no one can say when its first church was built. For miles around, Glastonbury Tor (14), rising 500 feet above sea-level, is a prominent landmark; on its summit stand the ruins of St Michael's Chapel, which was destroyed by subsidence in 1271 and rebuilt in the fifteenth century. The tower, probably a fourteenth-century survivor of the disaster, has two strange sculptured scenes over its portal; they represent St Michael weighing the souls of the departed, and, more prosaically, a woman milking a cow. Glastonbury is steeped in legend; some say that Joseph of Arimathaea is buried in St Catherine's Chapel in the parish church, and indeed the chapel contains a most remarkable tomb. There are other legends associating Glastonbury with King Arthur and his knights, but the story which has the greatest popular appeal concerns the Glastonbury Thorn. It is said that this tree is descended from the miraculous thorn planted by Joseph of Arimathaea when he came as a missionary to Britain. He pushed his staff into the ground on Wirral Hill and it burst into blossom. More certain is it that a church existed here at the beginning of the eighth century, and in Norman times more elaborate buildings were erected but were destroyed by fire shortly afterwards. The Abbey was begun in 1186 and dedicated in 1303, though 200 years were to pass before it was complete. Like other monastic properties the Abbey was destroyed at the Reformation and today only part of the walls of the nave still stand (15). They serve, however, to remind us of the spaciousness of the great church and the beautiful simplicity of its architecture. Of the other monastic buildings only the abbey tithe barn and the fine fifteenth-century abbot's kitchen remain.

Le Château de Nunney (13), à l'est de Somerset, entre Shepton Mallet et Frome fut construit sur le modèle de la Bastille en 1373. Au sommet de Glastonbury Tor (14) subsistent les ruines de la Chapelle St Michel dont le portail présente deux étranges sculptures: l'une, St Michel pesant les âmes des défunts, l'autre, une femme trayant une vache. Les légendes ici abondent sur le roi Arthur ou sur le « Buisson Épineux » de Glastonbury planté par Joseph d'Arimathie quand il vint comme missionnaire en Angleterre. D'autres édifices ont existé à l'époque normande, comme en témoignent les murs de la nef de l'Abbaye (15) détruite pendant la Réforme, mais dont on peut imaginer la magnifique simplicité de son architecture.

Nunney Castle (13) wurde von Sir John Delamere nach dem Vorbild der Bastille gebaut, aber während des Bürgerkrieges zerstört. Glastonbury Tor (14) ist eine weithin sichtbare Erhebung. Auf ihrem Gipfel stehen die Ruinen der St Michaelskapelle, die 1271 zerstört und im 15. Jh. wieder aufgebaut wurde. Über dem Turmportal ist St Michael dargestellt. Viele Legenden ranken sich um Glastonbury als eine der Wiegen des Christentums in England. Dort soll bereits im 8. Jh. eine Kirche gewesen sein. Mit dem Bau der Abtei wurde 1186 begonnen, aber es dauerte weitere fünf Jahrhunderte, bis sie beendet wurde. Heute sind von der Abtei nur noch die Mauern des Schiffs (15), die Scheune und Küche erhalten.

16

17

Montacute – the name is derived from a nearby hill 'Mons Acutus' – is chiefly known for Montacute House (16), a magnificent mansion dating from Elizabethan days. A feature of the estate is the fine gardens and pavilion. The house, built in the form of a letter 'H', is over 170 feet long. The interior is notable for its Long Gallery and for its Hall with a minstrel gallery. Yeovil, a thriving town on the borders of Somerset and Dorset, has long been known as a centre for the glove-making industry, but it has important engineering and aeronautical interests as well. Yeovil has several fine old inns, one of which, the George, a half-timbered building, still looks much as it did when it was built in Tudor days. The glory of Yeovil is its impressive Perpendicular church, the interior of which is extremely spacious. Wooded glades and a charming lake are attractive features of Nine Springs (17), one of the beauty spots of Yeovil. Somerset is rich in fine examples of domestic architecture, two of which are featured on these pages. Barrington Court (18), situated about four miles from Ilminster, was originally built at the beginning of the sixteenth century. The imposing exterior is largely original, but much of the internal decoration has been brought here from other houses. The grounds contain a sundial with ten faces. The mansion is now in the care of the National Trust. In Ilminster, the nearest town, which has had a market since Norman times, the tombs of Nicholas and Dorothy Wadham, the founders of Wadham College, Oxford, are in the church. Cothay Manor (19), situated in the west of the county near the Devon border, is a comparatively small mansion which dates from the end of the fifteenth century. Over the well-preserved Gatehouse appear the arms of the Bluet family who were the original owners.

Le magnifique manoir élisabétain de Montacute (16) construit en forme de H. L'intérieur est remarquable par sa Longue Galerie et son Hall avec la Galerie des Ménestrels. Nine Springs (17) est un des coins pittoresques de Yeovil, ville fleurissante au bord du Somerset et du Dorset, aux vieilles auberges et un centre important du gant. Barrington Court (18) construit au début du 16e siècle, près d'Ilminster où se trouvent les tombes de Nicolas et Dorothée Wadham, fondateurs du Wadham College d'Oxford. Le manoir de Cothay (19), fin du 15e siècle a une loge-de-garde avec les armes de la famille Bluet.

Montacute House (16) ist ein herrliches elisabethanisches Herrenhaus, umgeben von einem großen Park. Die lange Gallerie und die Halle sind besonders gelungen. Yeovil war lange ein Zentrum der Handschuhmacher. Viel besucht werden hier die alten Wirtshäuser, spätgotische Kirche und Nine Springs (17), eine versumpfte Niederung mit einem See. Ilminster ist ein alter normannischer Markt. Folgende sind zwei gute Beispiele der bürgerlichen Architektur Somersets; Barrington Court (18), nahe Ilminster, und Cothay Manor (19), nahe der Grenze zu Devon, wurden im 16. bzw. 15. Jh. gebaut.

18

19

Typique des paisibles scènes rurales du Somerset du Nord, ce cottage au bord de l'eau à Quantoxhead (20). Blue Anchor Bay (21) a des rochers d'albâtre et une plage riche en fossiles. Le château de Dunster (22) d'origine normande est un des rares à avoir été habité sans interruption depuis sa construction; parmi ses trésors, un escalier de chêne sculpté et un plafond du 17e siècle à caissons de cuir où sont peintes scènes d'Antoine et Cléopâtre. Le Yarn Market (23) à huit pignons datant du 17e siècle nous rappelle que Dunster fut autrefois renommé pour son commerce de draps.

Das am Wasser gelegene Cottage zu Quantoxhead (20) vermittelt ein typisches Bild des ländlichen Nordsomersets. Blue Anchor Bay (21) ist aus Alabastergestein, und der Strand ist reich an Fossilien. Die Geschichte von Dunster ist untrennbar mit seinem Schloß (22) verbunden. Es war ursprünglich eine normannische Gründung und ist fast ununterbrochen bewohnt worden. Die Burg beherbergt viele kunsthistorische Schätze. Das Wirtshaus Luttrel Arms ist nach dem Burgbesitzern benannt. Eine weitere Sehenswürdigkeit ist der Yarn Markt (23), ein Zeuge für das ehemals berühmte Fachgewerbe.

20

21

22

Typical of the peaceful rural scenes of northern Somerset is the waterside cottage at Quantoxhead (20). There are actually two villages of the name, West Quantoxhead on the Taunton–Minehead road, and East Quantoxhead nearer the coast. The latter has a Court House dating from the early seventeenth century. Blue Anchor Bay (21) is situated to the east of Minehead and has interesting alabaster rocks and a beach rich in fossils. A mile inland is Old Cleeve with a fine church on the site of a Saxon predecessor. The history of Dunster is inseparable from the history of its castle (22), overlooking the charming High Street which still retains something of the spirit of olden days. Dunster Castle was originally a Norman foundation, and part of the fortifications still remaining were built shortly after the Conquest. The present buildings, which have been much altered down the centuries, include some Tudor work. The castle is one of the few in England which have been lived in continuously almost since its foundation. Two families, the de Mohuns and the Luttrells, have been its owners. Among its treasures are a finely carved oak staircase, an intricate seventeenth-century plastered ceiling and leather panels, believed to be Spanish or Portuguese, on which are painted scenes from *Antony and Cleopatra*. From Dunster Park there is a fine view of Grabhurst – or Grabbist – Hill, with Dunkery Beacon away in the distance. Dunster Church was divided for monks and people at the end of the fifteenth century by a sixty-foot-long screen made by Flemish craftsmen. Many of the Luttrells have their last resting place here, including St Hugh Luttrell, the first of the family to inhabit the castle. The family is also commemorated by the Luttrell Arms, a fine old inn which retains several medieval features. The most interesting monument in the little town is, however, the eight-gabled Yarn Market (23), which dates from the seventeenth century and reminds us that Dunster was once renowned for its trade in cloth.

24

Minehead is both a deservedly popular holiday resort and a quaint old town, whose flower-decked thatched cottages are a constant delight to the many visitors. The firm golden sands and sea-front are sheltered by the wooded promontory called North Hill (24), from which delightful views may be enjoyed. Equally fine are the views from the churchyard of St Michael's Church (25) which dates from the fourteenth century and has a fine castellated tower. In olden times lights were kept burning in the church as a beacon for travellers on the moor and for ships making for the harbour, which was originally constructed in the seventeenth century and which was for many years second in importance to Bristol as a Channel port. The village of Selworthy lies a little way off the main road between Porlock and Minehead. It is one of the most frequented beauty spots of northern Somerset and must on no account be bypassed by the visitor who would see rural England at her very best. Old-world thatched cottages (26), beautifully sited on the slopes around the green, make Selworthy one of the most lovely villages in the whole of the country. Some of these houses are modern or modernised, some of them old, but none is as old as the fifteenth-century tithe-barn in the grounds of the rectory, and that, too, may not have been here when the church was first built at the top of the hill. From the churchyard the view extends as far as 1700-foot-high Dunkery Beacon on Exmoor. The domestic architecture of Somerset is particularly attractive. Thatch, limewashed walls, red-brick cottages with shingle roofs and buildings of local stone harmonise perfectly with the warm colours of the countryside. Typical of this pleasant building are the cottages at Allerford, a village close to Porlock. The most notable feature of the village is the twin-arched packhorse bridge (27), which has been here for hundreds of years. These packhorse bridges are indeed a feature of this part of the West Country; there is another well-preserved specimen, set in a delightful wooded glade, which spans the little River Avill at nearby Dunster.

North Hill (24), d'où l'on a une remarquable vue sur le front-de-mer doré de Minehead, à la fois station estivale et vieille ville pittoresque. L'église St Michel (25) du 14e siècle, au beau clocher crénelé, restait autrefois éclairée toute la nuit servant ainsi de fanal aux voyageurs et aux bateaux. Ne manquez pas, sur la route de Porlock à Minehead, l'adorable village rural de Selworthy, un des coins les plus appréciés du Somerset du nord, avec ses cottages chapeautés de chaume (26). A Alleford, près de Porlock, un pont à double arcade pour les bêtes de somme (27), vieux de plusieurs centaines d'années.

Der Strand des bezaubernden Ferienortes Minehead ist durch eine hügelige Landzunge, dem North Hill (24) geschützt. Von der St Michaelskirche (25) aus dem 14. Jh. hat man einen schönen Landblick. Das Dorf Selworthy, zwischen Porlock und Minehead gelegen, ist ein ländliches Kleinod. Besonders sehenswert sind die strohgedeckten Cottages (26), aber auch die vierhundert Jahre alte Zehntscheune. Die Landschaft und Architektur bilden in Somerset ein harmonisches und farbenfrohes Ganzes; Gut erhalten sind die doppelbogigen Packpferdbrücken. in Allerford (27) und Dunster.

25

26

27

Porlock means 'the enclosed harbour' and was once a port, but today the town lies more than a mile from the Bristol Channel. It has still, however, a maritime link, curiously named Porlock Weir (28), where a bar of shingle has facilitated the construction of a tiny harbour, the most picturesque little haven in the county. Porlock lies at the foot of the wooded slopes of Exmoor and has several old inns, among them the Ship, where the poet Southey once stayed. The Church of St Dubricius has a number of effigied tombs, some of them dating from the twelfth century, and is particularly rich in ornamentation. The church lacks its spire, which local legend says was blown away in a gale and used to complete the church at Culbone, reputedly the smallest church in England. Porlock Hill is well known to motorists, for it is one of the steepest in the country, the maximum gradient being 1 in 4. The hill can, however, be avoided by using an alternative toll-road. The heart of Exmoor was once a great forest, but today, although the area is more wooded than Dartmoor, large tracts are true moorland covered with heather, bracken and grass. Here is the only place in England where red deer still roam free. Before 1815 the whole of Exmoor belonged to the Crown, but today it is a National Park. The beautiful thatched cottages and air of yesterday of Luccombe (29) have contributed to its description of the ideal Exmoor village. The church, which has a charming lych-gate and a fine perpendicular tower, contains a number of interesting monuments, including one to a former rector, Henry Byam. He was a staunch supporter of Charles I, and he raised a troop for the royalist army in which four of his sons served as officers. Luccombe has a picturesque situation at the foot of Dunkery Beacon and the village is in the care of the National Trust. From the top of the 1700-foot-high Beacon there are fine views over Exmoor towards Dartmoor. A short way to the south of Wheddon Cross and just off the main road lies the village of Winsford, astride the upper reaches of the Exe. The village still has its old packhorse bridge and among its attractive buildings is the Royal Oak (30), a delightful thatched inn. The church contains the Royal Arms of James I. Winsford Hill, to the south-west, is a notable viewpoint.

Porlock signifie « le port enmuré » car il se trouve aujourd'hui à plus d'un mille du Bristol Channel. Il garde cependant un lien maritime. Porlock Weir (28) où une traverse de galets a facilité la construction d'un minuscule port, le plus pittoresque du comté. Porlock, au pied des pentes boisées de l'Exmoor, a plusieurs vieilles auberges, parmi lesquelles « the Ship » où descendit le poète Southey. L'église St Dubricius perdit sa flèche, d'après les légendes locales, un jour de rafales. Celle-ci aurait servi à compléter l'église de Culbone, réputée la plus petite d'Angleterre. Les beaux cottages aux toits de chaume de Luccombe, considéré comme le village idéal de l'Exmoor (29). Winsford, au sud de Wheddon Cross, a encore son vieux pont à bêtes de somme et entre autres une délicieuse auberge (30) à toit chaumé.

Porlock, früher eine Hafenstadt mit Zugang zur See, liegt heute eine Meile vom Bristolkanal entfernt und ist nur durch Porlock Weir (28) mit dem Meer verbunden. Sehenswert sind der malerische Hafen und die St Dubriciuskirche. In dem Kirchfriedhof findet man viele sehr sehr alte Grabsteine. In Culbone steht die kleinste Kirche Englands. Hinter Porlock beginnt das Exmoor, das heute ein Nationalpark ist. Heute sind weite Flächen mit Heide, Farnkraut und Gras bestanden, auf denen Rottier frei umherzieht. Luccombe (29), am Fuße des Dunkery Beacon gelegen, ist ein wunderschönes Exmoordorf mit vielen alten Gebäuden. Südlich von Wheddon Cross liegt Winsford mit seiner alten Packpferdbrücke und dem strohgedeckten Wirtshaus „Royal Oak" (30).

31

32

Tarr Steps (31) est un pont vieux d'au moins 900 ans, de 180 pieds de long sur la rivière Barle, non loin de Dulverton. Withypool (32), charmant village également situé sur le Barle, est un lieu populaire de pêche à la ligne. Au confluent du Lyn et du Badgworthy Water, à Oare, se trouve l'eglise (33) où l'héroïne du roman *Lorna Doone* de Blackmore est blessée le jour de ses noces devant l'autel. L'auteur séjourne dans cette région mais sa description de la Doone Valley (34) a été empruntée à plusieurs combes de l'Exmoor, région où les promenades à poney (35) connaissent une vogue croissante.

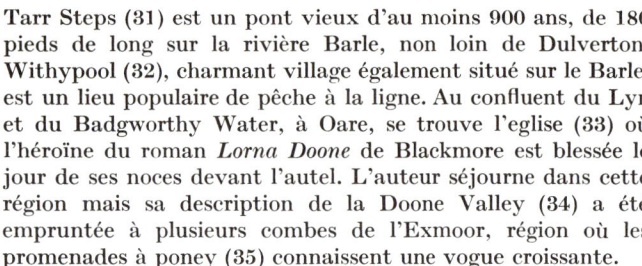

Die kleine Klopferbrücke, Tarr Steps (31) genannt, überquert die Barle nicht weit von Dulverton und soll etwa 900 Jahre alt sein. Withypool (32), ebenfalls an der Barle, gelegen, ist ein Zentrum für Angler. Auf dem Hügel oberhalb des Dorfes befindet sich ein Steinring aus der Bronzezeit. Das Dorf und besonders die Kirche von Oare (33), als auch das Doone-Tal (34), haben du durch den Roman *Lorna Doone* von Blackmore Bekanntheit erlangt. Um das Exmoor wirklich kennenzulernen, sollte man entweder weite Wanderungen machen oder mit dem Pony ausreiten (35).

33

34

Tarr Steps (31) is a clapper bridge which, with its approaches, measures 180 feet in length. It crosses the River Barle nor far from Dulverton and has been here, it is believed, for at least 900 years. It is a mute witness to the skill of its builders that it has for so long survived the winter floods. Withypool (32), a charming Exmoor village, is also situated on the Barle, some miles above Tarr Steps. It is a popular angling centre. On the hill overlooking the village is a stone circle of the Bronze Age. Badgworthy Water, a tributary of the Lyn, forms the actual boundary between Somerset and Devon for much of its course. A mile to the west of the confluence of the two streams we come to the village of Oare; the church (33) plays a prominent part in the story of *Lorna Doone*, for the heroine was shot here by Carver Doone on her wedding day, as she stood at the altar with John Ridd. Blackmore lived at the Royal Oak Inn while he was engaged on this book. Many of the author's locations can be identified with places on Exmoor, but it is probable that his description of the Doone Valley (34) is a composite one, with details drawn from several of the Exmoor combes. Although Blackmore's Doones were fictional characters, there is evidence that in the seventeenth century Exmoor was indeed the haunt of outlaws who terrorised the peaceable farmer and waylaid the lonely traveller. Today Exmoor is safe country, to be explored ideally on foot or on horseback, and indeed pony-trekking (35) is yearly increasing in popularity, but however he travels, the visitor is never far from the welcome of pleasant townships.

Noss Mayo (36), beautifully situated on the estuary of the River Yealm.
Noss Mayo (36) a une belle situation sur l'estuaire du Yealm.
Noss Mayo (36) an der Yealm-mündung schön gelegen.

Devon

Glorious Devon is famed far beyond these islands for its incomparable loveliness. The name is derived from a Celtic word which means 'the land of deep valleys', but it is not only the valleys, lovely though they are, which express the whole personality of the county. The coasts, the moors, the rich red soil, the many varieties of bird, animal and plant life, and the fascinating old legends, all play their part in making Devon the wonderful region that it is. Like Cornwall, Devon has two coasts separated by the uplands of Dartmoor and Exmoor. The northern coast extends along the shore of the Bristol Channel and the Atlantic, and includes the wide sweep of Bideford Bay and the popular resorts of Ilfracombe and Lynmouth. The southern coast, stretching from Seaton, on the Dorset border, to Plymouth, is a succession of delightful bays, coves and headlands. The rivers of South Devon are exquisitely beautiful, yet each is in some indefinable way different from all the others. On the southern coast are some of the finest seaside resorts in the West, offering the visitor everything he or she could want for the ideal holiday. A considerable part of the south and west of Devon is occupied by the great granite upland of Dartmoor. Much of the northern part of Dartmoor is marshy, but the fen is often concealed by beautiful mosses, and it is only near the 'mires', which are found chiefly near the sources of streams, that especial care is necessary. The tors, the most important natural feature of Dartmoor, are the outcrops of granite generally to be found at the very tops of the hills, the word 'tor' being Celtic for tower. Although the greater part of Exmoor lies in Somerset, the extreme western area is in the county of Devon. Exmoor was once a great forest, but today, although the area is more wooded than Dartmoor, large tracts are true moorland, covered with heather, bracken and grass. From the moor many narrow valleys lead down to the sea; they bear the attractive West-country name of 'combes'. On both Exmoor and Dartmoor many relics of prehistoric times have been discovered.

37

The rivers East and West Lyn, tumbling down their respective combes, unite and find their way into the sea at Lynmouth (37), a haunt of artists and photographers and one of the most charming places in England. In 1952 tragedy struck when the river overflowed and brought rocks and swirling water rushing down through the little town. The sister village of Lynton is situated 500 feet high on the cliffs to the west of Lynmouth and is linked to the latter by a funicular railway, operated by water power. On the quayside stands the curiously shaped Rhenish Tower, the original of which was built over a century ago in order to act as a beacon for the harbour. This tower was destroyed in the 1952 floods but a successor once more graces the quayside. The Trentishoe Hills, which cradle the little River Heddon and its tributaries, figure in two of Blackmore's romances of the region. The scenery is extremely fine, with wide tracts of wooded moorland and fine cliffs. From Lynton the approach is through the Valley of Rocks; a diversion from the Martinhoe road brings the visitor to Woody Bay down a typical Devon combe with a rushing stream. From Woody Bay there is a breathtaking drive along the cliffs to Combe Martin, passing Heddon's Mouth (38), a charming cove at the mouth of the River Heddon, a notable trout stream. Many who have spent a rewarding time exploring the little glens and valleys of the region stop at Hunter's Inn (39), a charming hostelry which seems to belong to the landscape and not to intrude upon it. Combe Martin (40) is named after one of William the Conqueror's followers, and the Church of St Peter ad Vincula was originally built shortly after the Norman Conquest. Its principal feature of interest is a carved wooden screen dating from the fifteenth century. Whoever made it must have been a careless craftsman, for the central doors are too wide for the opening and cannot be closed. One of the most curious features of Combe Martin is a hotel known as the Pack of Cards. It is said to have been built with the proceeds of gambling and to have been designed to resemble a pack of cards.

Lynmouth (37), où confluent les Lyn de l'Est et de l'Ouest, avec ses cottages et son pittoresque front-de-mer, est un des lieux les plus charmants d'Angleterre, fréquenté par les artistes et les photographes. A Woody Bay, prenez la route le long des falaises, vous en aurez le souffle coupé, jusqu'à Combe Martin (40), en passant la délicieuse anse de Heddon's Mouth (38) connez pour ses truites. Après avoir exploré les clairières et les vallées de la région, arrêtez-vous à Hunter's Inn (39), charmante hostellerie qui semble appartenir au paysage plutôt que de s'y surajouter.

Die Flüsse East und West Lyn münden bei Lynmouth (37) in die See. Das Nachbardorf Lynton liegt auf einem 120 m hohen Kliff und ist mit Lynmouth durch eine Drahtseilbahn verbunden. Der Rhenish Tower war vor hundert Jahren ein Leuchtturm. Die Trentishoe Hills sind das Quellgebiet für den Haddon, einen guten Forellenbach. Folgen wir der Küste weiter, so kommen wir nach Woody Bay, Combe Martin (40) mit einer normannischen Kirche und Heddon's Mouth (38), einer kleinen Bucht. In Hunter's Inn (39) lohnt es sich nach einem Ausflug in die Umgebung Rast zu machen.

38

39

40

41

Ilfracombe is not only the leading resort of North Devon, it is also the oldest, and offers a considerable variety of holiday amenities. The most striking impression of the town is undoubtedly gained when the visitor arrives by sea, for the harbour (41) has a strangely continental aspect and many visitors find its constant activity fascinating. On the west side of the pier is Lantern Rock, on which there is a lighthouse converted from a 700-year-old chapel, dedicated to St Nicholas. The Capstone, perhaps the most outstanding landmark of Ilfracombe rises precipitously from the sea to a height of over 150 feet. Woolacombe (42) has grown in stature as a seaside resort largely on account of its wonderful sandy beach, some three miles in length and a paradise for the young. It lies at the foot of a combe and, although it faces the Atlantic, is nevertheless sheltered from the north and east, so the air is bracing without being unduly blustery. Woolacombe Bay is separated from Croyde Bay by Baggy Point with the little inlet of Combesgate Beach (43) tucked away in the shelter of the rocky cliffs, in which there are a number of caves, the largest of which, called Baggy Hole, is usually only accessible by boat. Baggy Point was presented by its former owner to the National Trust. A little way inland lies the interesting village of Georgeham (44) with an old church now rebuilt. Croyde Bay (45) is in the parish of Georgeham and is an excellent place for a family holiday. Through the village, which is mentioned in Domesday Book as Crideholda, the Croyde stream flows alongside the road.

42

44

43

Ilfracombe est non seulement le centre de villégiature de pointe du Devon du Nord, c'est aussi le plus ancien. Son port (41) à l'incessante activité, a un aspect étrangement continental sur Lantern Rock, une chapelle vieille de 700 ans a été convertie en phare. Wollacombe (42) est une station balnéaire en essor grâce à sa merveilleuse plage sablonneuse longue de près de 3 milles. Combesgate Beach (43) se cache dans des falaises trouées de grottes. Georgeham (44) est un village intéressant pourvu d'une vieilles église reconstruite. Croyde Bay (45) est un excellent endroit pour passer des vacances familiales.

Ilfracombe ist der älteste und zugleich führende Ferienort in Norddevon. Den besten Eindruck von der Stadt bekommt der Besucher im Hafen (41). Auf der westen Seite des Hafendammes erhebt sich Lantern Rock, auf dem ein Leuchtturm steht. Noch höher als dieser ist der steil aufragende Capstone. Woolacombe (42) hat einen herrlichen drei Meilen langen Sandstrand. Combesgate Beach (43) liegt versteckt zwischen Kliffs nahe Baggy Point. Etwas landeinwärts befindet sich Georgeham (44) mit einer alten Kirche. Croyde Bay (45), wo der Croyde-bach in die See mündet, ist ideal für Ferien.

45

Barnstaple, soi disant la ville la plus vieille d'Angleterre, a quelques industries de dentelle, ganterie, poterie et est le centre d'une fleurissante région agricole. Son architecture est très belle: pont à 16 arches du 13ᵉ siècle, Flèche en spinale de l'église St Pierre, colonnade de Queen Anne's Walk (46). Westward Ho! dont le nom vient d'un roman de Kingsley a une excellent plage (47). A 11 milles de Bideford l'adorable village de Clovelly est constitué d'une seule rue à pic bordée de cottages fleuris (48). Hartland Point (49) ou « Promontoire d'Hercule », à 120 pieds au-dessus de la mer.

Barnstaple nimmt in Anspruch, die älteste Marktstadt in diesem Gebiet zu sein und seine Geschichte geht bis in sächsische Zeiten zurück. Barnstaple ist reich an schönen Bauwerken, wie z.B. den Penrose Armenhäusern, der St Peterkirche und Queen Anne's Walk (46). Zu Westward Ho! befindet sich das United Services College, wo Kipling zur Schule ging; der Strand (47) ist ausgezeichnet zum Wellenreiten. Die Hauptstraße von Clovelly (48) ist so steil, daß Esel die Beförderung der Gäste übernehmen müssen. Hartland Point (49) ist der äußerste nordwestliche Punkt von Devon.

46

47

48

Barnstaple claims to be the oldest borough in the country, and it has certainly been a considerable town since Saxon days. It has a number of small industries, including the making of lace, gloves and pottery, and it is the centre of a thriving agricultural district. The River Taw is crossed by a bridge of sixteen arches which dates originally from the thirteenth century. Barnstaple is particularly rich in fine architecture; of special interest are the Penrose Almshouses, built in the seventeenth century. The most striking feature of the Parish Church of St Peter is its twisted spire. Queen Anne's Walk (46) is an impressive colonnade, with fine sculptures crowned by a statue of Queen Anne. Westward Ho! which takes its name from Kingsley's novel, was developed in the latter half of the nineteenth century. In 1874 the United Services College was established here and is the setting of Kipling's *Stalky and Co.*, based on the author's schooldays. Surfing from the excellent beach (47) is a popular pastime. A curious feature of the shore is a pebble ridge which forms a natural sea-wall. The northern coast of Devon, along the Bristol Channel, abounds in picturesque seaside villages, and none is fairer than Clovelly, perhaps the most frequented spot in the whole of this part of the county. Clovelly (48) is reached from Bideford, from which it is but eleven miles distant, but vehicles must be parked at the entrance to the village, which consists of one steep street flanked by gay flower-decked cottages. This 'main street', bearing the quaint name of 'Down-a-long', is too steep for wheeled traffic and so the willing donkey is often pressed into service as a means of transport. The early prosperity of Clovelly is due in no small measure to the Cary family who figure, with their village, in Kingsley's *Westward Ho!* Dickens, too, described Clovelly in *A Message from the Sea*. Named by Ptolemy 'The Promontory of Hercules', Hartland Point (49) forms the extreme north-westerly point of Devon. The most important features of Hartland Point are the coastguard station on the top of the cliffs and the lighthouse perched on a ledge some 120 feet above the sea. About twelve miles offshore is Lundy Island, a volcanic rock which is privately owned and which is of great interest to the naturalist. Numerous sea-birds breed there, including the cormorant and puffin, and there are deer, sheep and wild goats. In bygone days Lundy Island was often used as a base by smugglers and pirates. Today it is a popular destination for summer excursions.

Bickleigh (50) on the left bank of the River Exe near Tiverton, is a village with charming thatched buildings, a fifteenth-century castle with some Norman work still remaining, and a church which contains memorials to the Carew family. Exeter, the county town and university city of Devon, has much of interest to offer the visitor. First and foremost is its fine cathedral, which has no central tower, so that the splendour of the interior in Decorated style and the Perpendicular east window can be fully appreciated. The West Front (51) is a splendid example of fourteenth-century architecture. The two Norman towers house a peal of fourteen bells; thirteen are in the south tower and the largest, 'Great Peter', on which curfew is sounded every evening, in the other. Honiton in the west of the county is noted for its lace manufacture; in the neighbourhood are many charming thatched cottages, such as the one featured on this page (52). Where the red sandstone cliffs of Devon's southern coast begin to give way to chalk, we find Seaton (53), pleasantly situated on the west bank of the estuary of the River Axe. Perhaps the word 'estuary' is not particularly accurate, for the Axe enters the sea through a pebble bar. The river, however, is popular with fishermen, for both salmon and trout can be caught in its waters. Beer (54) lies in the lee of the imposing headland called Beer Head, the most westerly chalk promontory in the country. Lace, made in the village, was used for Queen Victoria's wedding dress, and from several quarries in the neighbourhood came the freestone which was used in the building of Exeter Cathedral. Sidmouth (55) has grown up where the little River Sid rather impertinently pushes its way into the sea between the towering cliffs of Peak Hill, on the west, and Salcombe Hill to the east. A well-designed promenade has contributed to the development of this popular resort, which has a remarkably equable climate. The Duke of York, the father of the future Queen Victoria, died here in 1820.

50

51

52

Bickleigh (50), sur la rive gauche de l'Exe près de Tiverton, a un château du 15e siècle avec des empreintes de style normand. La Façade ouest de la cathédrale d'Exeter (51) est un remarquable exemple d'architecture de 14e siècle; ses deux clochers abritent 14 cloches dont la plus grosse « Great Peter » sert à sonner le couvre-feu chaque soir. Charmant cottage chapeauté de chaume (52), aux environs de Honiton. Seaton (53) est agréablement situé sur les bords ouest de l'estuaire de l'Axe, rivière abondante en truites et en saumons. Protégé par un imposant promontoire, Beer (54) est connu pour sa dentelle qui servit à la confection de la robe de mariée de la reine Victoria. La station balnéaire de Sidmouth (55) est dominée par les promontoires de Peak Hill et de Salcombe Hill.

In Bickleigh (50), an der Exe nahe Tiverton gelegen, findet der Besucher eine Burg aus dem 15. Jh. Von hier ist es nicht weit nach Exeter, der Lands- und Universitätsstadt von Devon. Im Baustil der Kathedrale (51) verbinden sich Elemente aus normannischer Zeit und dem 14. Jh. Vom Nordturm wird jeden Tag die Abendglocke geläutet. Honiton ist bekannt für seine Spitzenherstellung. In seiner Nachbarschaft gibe es viele schöne strohgedeckte Cottages wie dieses (52). Dort, wo der rote Sandstein in Kreide übergeht, liegt Seaton (53), das von Anglern geschätzt wird. Aus den Steinbrüchen in der Umgebung von Beer (54) kamen die Bausteine für die Kathedrale von Exeter. Die Spitzen an Königin Viktorias Hochzeits Kleid werden ebenfalls hier hergestellt. Sidmouth (55) liegt geschützt zwischen den Kliffs von Peak Hill und Salcombe Hill.

Ladram Bay (56), some three miles south-west of Sidmouth, is best approached over Peak Hill, from which one enjoys a delightful view of the huge masses of sandstone which have become detached from the cliffs owing to the action of the sea and which bear the quaint name of the 'Picket Rocks'. Innumerable sea-birds nest in these rocks and in the impressive sandstone cliffs. Similar red cliffs shelter Sandy Bay at Exmouth (57), to which it is possible to walk from the town around Orcombe Point at low tide. Exmouth has been a notable resort for a long time, and it possesses a small but busy harbour. The docks were built in the last century and opened in 1869. In the fourteenth century the town provided ships and seamen for Edward III's expedition to Calais. From the Maer, a stretch of sloping sandy ground leading to Orcombe Point, there are fine views of the estuary and the coast beyond. Dawlish (58) lies a little way to the east, between the estuaries of the Exe and Teign. Here the railway runs right beside the sea, and the railway station is almost literally 'on the beach'. Dawlish Water flows through the town and helps to keep the temperature pleasantly cool in summer. An intensely interesting stretch of coast to the south-east of the town, known as 'the Warren', is noted for its wild-bird life. Teignmouth is, after Exmouth, the oldest seaside town in Devon. It lies on the east side of the estuary of the River Teign and is joined to Sheldon on the opposite bank by an iron bridge, which was opened in 1931 and replaced a former wooden structure. The estuary is navigable for small craft, but care is needed, as there are extensive sandbanks. Teignmouth still builds yachts and has interests in the export of local fireclays. A feature of the sea-front is the 'Den' (59), a large expanse of lawns and flowerbeds backed by a crescent of Regency houses. The Perpendicular Church of St James has an octagonal lantern and a fine fourteenth-century carved stone reredos. Although it is administratively part of Teignmouth, Shaldon still retains much of its former village atmosphere. There are a few Regency houses and a remarkable modern church, St Peter's, much praised for its imaginative architecture. Along the shore the rocks have been eroded into curious shapes, said to resemble 'parsons', 'bishops' and 'toads'.

56

57

58

59

Ladram Bay (56), à quelques 3 milles au sud-ouest de Sidmouth, se doit d'être approché par Peak Hill d'où l'on a une remarquable vue sur d'énormes blocs de grès, détachés des falaises par la mer, et connus sous le nom de « Picket Rocks ». Exmouth (57) est un petit port très actif qui fournit au 14e siècle les navires et les équipages pour l'expédition d'Édouard III vers Calais. Dawlish (58), a sa gare presque littéralement sur la plage. Le « Den » (59) avec ses pelouses, parterres fleuris et maisons Régence à Teignmouth, la plus ancienne station balnéaire du Devon après Exmouth.

Der beste Weg nach Ladram Bay (56) führt über Peak Hill. Rote Sandsteinkliffs schützen Sandy Bay bei Exmouth (57) einem kleinen aber geschäftigen Hafen. In Dawlish (58) verlaufen die Eisenbahngleise fast buchstäblich auf dem Strand. The Warren, südöstlich von der Stadt, ist ein Vogelparadies. Teignmouth die zweitälteste Stadt Küstenstadt Devons, ist mit Shaldon an der anderen Seite der Teignmündung durch eine eiserne Brücke verbindet. In Teignmouth werden immer noch Yachten gebaut. Eine Besonderheit ist der „Den" (59), eine weite halbkreisförmige Rasenfläche.

60

61

North Bovey (60) a une auberge célèbre « the Ring of Bells » et une belle église. Les poneys (61) sont l'une des grandes attractions du Dartmoor, et s'approchent de vous dans l'espoir d'une friandise. A Postbridge est le plus bel exemple d'ancien pont du Devon (62), aussi stable que lorsqu'il fut construit plusieurs siècles auparavant. Les Dart de l'Est et de l'Ouest confluent à Badger's Holt, Dartmeet (63), pour former le Dart. Buckfast Abbey (64), fondée en 1030, puis détruite en grande partie pendant la Dissolution, fut rachetée et reconstruite par des Bénédictins français. Burrator Reservoir (65) est un agréable lac artificiel aux pieds de Sheepstor.

North Bovey (60) ist ein reizendes Dorf im Dartmoor mit einem bekannten Wirtshaus und einer spätgotischen Kirche aus Granit. Die Dartmoor-Poneys (61) sind eine der größten Attraktionen des Moors. Eine der besten Klopferbrücken in Devon steht in Postbridge (62). Der Dart ist einer der schönsten Flüsse der britischen Inseln. Der Ost- und Westdart vereinigen sich bei Badger's Holt, Dartmeet (63), Buckfast Abbey (64), 1030 gegründet, wurde von König Canute gestiftet. Französische Benediktiner folgten den Zisterziensern und errichteten die heutige Kirche. Burrator-Reservoir (65) ist ein künstlicher aber anziehender See.

62

64

63

North Bovey (60) is one of the most charming villages of the Dartmoor region. It has a famous inn, the Ring of Bells, and a fine granite Perpendicular church in which the screen with its statuettes is of particular interest. The stone cross on the village green was once used as a footbridge over the River Bovey. Dartmoor ponies (61) are one of the great attractions of the Moor. Although well able to fend for themselves, they approach stationary vehicles on the Moorland roads and even in the villages, in the hope of a tit-bit. Postbridge is right in the middle of Dartmoor. Close to its seventeenth-century granite bridge, which carries the main road over the East Dart, is the finest example of a clapper bridge in Devon (62). Each of the granite spans joining the rough piers is about fifteen feet long, and the bridge is as safe today as when it was built many centuries ago. The River Dart is acknowledged to be one of the most beautiful rivers in the whole of the British Isles. Two streams, the East and West Darts, unite at Badger's Holt, Dartmeet (63) to form the main river, which becomes navigable for small craft at Totnes. Buckfast Abbey (64) was founded in 1030 and endowed by King Canute. After a temporary eclipse the abbey was revived by the Cistercians in the twelfth century but at the Dissolution the greater part of the buildings were destroyed. In 1882 French Benedictines bought the site and began in 1906 to erect the present church, a task which took them more than a quarter of a century. Burrator Reservoir (65) is an attractive artificial lake at the foot of Sheeps Tor near Yelverton.

66

67

68

A Torquay, la station la plus importante du Devon du Sud, le port (66) a un petit air italien avec toutes ses maisons blanches perchées sur les collines du Waldon et du Vane. Redgate Beach et Anstey's Cove (67) sont des plages isolées au nord-est du promontoire du Hope's Nose. Cockington (68) a gardé son charme d'autrefois avec ses cottages pittoresques et sa forge si souvent photographiée. Une belle plage sablonneuse et une moderne Salle des Fêtes (69) sont parmi les attraits de Paignton, fleurissante station balnéaire doublée d'un centre de navigation de plaisance et de pêche. Brixham (70) où fut construit la première *Mayflower*, accueillit Guillaume d'Orange quand il accepta la Couronne anglaise en 1688. Une statue sur le quai commémore cet événement. Stoke Gabriel (71) dont la beauté naturelle est rehaussée par son église.

Torquay, der führende Ferienort in Süddevon, ist einmalig schön gelegen. Um voll in den Zauber Torquays zu kommen, sollte man auf dem Seewege dorthin fahren. Der Hafen (66) und die weißen Häuser werden eingerahmt von den Waldon und Vane Hügeln. Auf der nordöstlichen Seite des Vorgebirges findet man eine Zahl von abgeschlossenen Stränden, darunter so schöne wie Redgate Beach und Anstey's Cove (67). Cockington (68) hat seinen Reiz über die Jahre erhalten können. Die Schmiede ist eines der Lieblingsmotive für Fotografen. Ein feiner Sandstrand und die moderne Festival Hall (69) sind zwei der anziehenden Merkmaler von Paignton. Brixham (70) war bis letzte Jh. größer als Plymouth. Hier wurde die erste *Mayflower* gebaut. Stoke Gabriel (71) liegt in einer friedlichen Bucht an den Ufern des Flusses Dart.

Torquay, the leading resort of south Devon, has a magnificent situation on the promontory which guards the northern end of Torbay. If a visitor should chance to see Torquay Harbour (66) from the sea for the first time, he might be forgiven for believing that here is an Italian scene, for behind the harbour Waldon and Vane Hills frame the water with clusters of white buildings. The harbour, which consists of an outer and an inner basin, owes its construction to the foresight of Lord Haldon, a member of the Palk family. On the north-eastern side of the promontory, known as Hope's Nose, are a number of secluded beaches, among them Redgate Beach and Anstey's Cove (67). The village of Cockington (68), now incorporated in the Borough of Torquay, still retains its old-world charm and is justly famous as the perfect example of a Devon village. Among the picturesque thatched cottages stands the forge at the corner, one of the most photographed buildings in the West. Nearby is Cockington Court, the former home of the Mallock family. The flourishing seaside resort of Paignton boasts a small harbour which was used commercially until the beginning of the present century. Now the harbour is used exclusively for pleasure and fishing craft. A fine sandy beach and a modern Festival Hall (69) are among the many attractive features of Paignton. In addition to its fame of having been larger than Plymouth until the latter years of the last century, Brixham (70) has other links with the premier seaport of Devon, for the first *Mayflower* was built here, as was her replica in our time. Brixham was the first to greet William of Orange when he came to accept the English Crown in 1688. A statue on the quay commemorates this event. The River Dart is undoubtedly one of the loveliest rivers in England, and beside the river or one of its numerous creeks lie peaceful little townships. Such a place is Stoke Gabriel (71), where a fine Perpendicular church with a restored screen enhances the natural beauty of the village.

69

70

71

For those who shun the bustle of more popular resorts and prefer simpler pleasures, such riverside villages as Dittisham (72) on the right bank of the Dart are of particular appeal. A feature of the fifteenth-century church is a modern carved pulpit. The estuary of the Dart was formerly protected by two castles, Kingswear Castle on the eastern and Dartmouth Castle (73) on the western shore. Close to the latter, which, like its counterpart, dates from Tudor times, stands the Church of St Petrox, which is principally a seventeenth-century building. Famous today as the home of the Royal Naval College, Dartmouth has always had close links with the sea, and the town has a particular attraction for yachtsmen, for whom the River Dart and the nearby Channel offer excellent sailing. South of the estuary of the Dart the main road from Dartmouth to Kingsbridge closely follows the shore of Start Bay as far as Torcross (74), situated at the end of the three-mile stretch of shingle and sand which is called Slapton Sands. The sands divide the sea from Slapton Ley, a natural freshwater lake noted for its bird life. American forces used this area as a training ground during the Second World War and an obelisk commemorates the event. In former times the Kingsbridge Estuary was of some commercial importance, and both Kingsbridge (75) and Salcombe were busy seaports. Kingsbridge, at the head of the long and complex estuary, has had a long history; its name commemorates a tenth-century bridge which joined two royal estates on either side of the river. There are several buildings dating from Tudor days still standing. Kingsbridge was famous, too, for its 'white ale', a beverage reputed to have been particularly potent. From East Portlemouth there is a fine view of Salcombe (76) near the seaward end of the estuary. Henry VIII built a castle here as part of the defences of the south coast, but only one tower remains today. Salcombe, a favoured yachting centre, enjoys an excellent climate, and sub-tropical plants flourish in the open.

72

73

74

75

Pour ceux qui fuient les stations trop fréquentées, les villages riverains comme celui de Dittisham (72) sur le Dart, avec son église du 15e siècle, sont d'un attrait particulier. L'estuaire du Dart est dominé par deux châteaux, Kingswear sur la rive droite et Dartmouth (73) sur la rive gauche. Torcross (74) se situe à l'extrémité d'une étendue de sable et de galets connue sous le nom de Slapton Sands. Kingsbridge (75) à l'entrée d'un long et complexe estuaire, était célèbre autrefois pour sa « bière blanche ». D'East Portlemouth, on a une très belle vue sur Salcombe (76) où Henri VIII fit construire un château dont il ne reste aujourd'hui plus qu'une tour.

Für jene, welche Ruhe wichtiger ist als das Getriebe der volkstümlicheren Badeorte, sind Dörfer wie Dittisham (72) ideal. Die Mündung des Dart wurde früher von Kingswear Castle und Dartmouth Castle (73) geschützt. Beide stammen aus Tudorzeiten. Dartmouth ist als Sitz des Royal Naval College bekannt. Die Hauptverkehrsstraße von Dartmouth nach Kingsbridge folgt der Küste bis Torcross (74), das am Rand der Slapton Sands liegt. Die Sande haben einen Frischwassersee, Slapton Ley, vom Meer abgetrennt. In früheren Zeiten waren die Häfen von Salcombe (76) und Kingsbridge (75) von großer Bedeutung. Die Name Kingsbridge ist abgeleitet von einer Brücke, die im 10. Jh. beide Flußufer verband.

Hope Cove (77), village de pêcheurs est un endroit idéal pour passer des vacances tranquilles; et les promenades sur les falaises avoisinantes sont les plus belles d'Angleterre. Une arche naturelle en pierre, une vieille église avec des fonts normands et des cottages typiques du Devon (78) sont quelques-uns des charmes de Thurlestone. Au sud-est de Plymouth situé dans une crique de l'estuaire du Yealm, Newton Ferrers (79) est parfois décrit comme le plus beau site du Devon. Wembury (80) se trouve au nord de l'estuaire du Yealm. Plymouth (81), la plus grande ville du Devon, très endommagée pendant la dernière guerre, a été reconstruite.

Die Küste im äußersten Süden Devons, der Streifen zwischen Bolt Head und Bolt Tail, ist ausgesprochen schön. Hope Cove (77), ein kleines Fischerdorf, ist ein geeigneter Ausgangspunkt für Wanderungen entlang der Kliffs. Die Sehenswürdigkeiten von Thurlestone sind der natürliche Felsenbogen, die alte Kirche und die vielen typischen Devon-cottages (78). Südöstlich von Plymouth liegt Newton Ferrers (79), von dem gesagt wird, es habe die schönste Lage in Devon. Stolz erhebt sich die Heiligkreuzkirche über den Cottages. An dem Yealm liegt Wembury (80). Plymouth (81) ist die größte Stadt in Devon. Am Hoe steht der Leuchtturm Smeaton's Tower.

78

79
80

The coast in the extreme south of Devon is particularly attractive, especially the stretch between Bolt Head on the western extremity of the Kingsbridge Estuary and Bolt Tail which forms the southern boundary of Bigbury Bay, on a rocky inlet of which lies Hope Cove (77), a fishing village and an attractive place for a quiet holiday. The cliff walks in the vicinity are unsurpassed in England. Further round the bay is Thurlestone, where there is a natural rock arch. Among the attractions of this charming village are a fine old church with a Norman font and some typical Devon cottages (78). To the south-east of Plymouth, exquisitely situated on a creek of the estuary of the River Yealm is Newton Ferrers (79), sometimes described as the village with the finest setting in Devon. Standing proudly above the charming cottages of the village is the fifteenth-century tower of the Church of Holy Cross. On the other side of the inlet is quaintly named Noss Mayo. On the north side of the Yealm Estuary, Wembury (80) is notable as the place from which came the Galsworthy family of *Forsyte Saga* fame. Plymouth (81), Devon's largest town, is situated between the estuaries of the Tamar and the Plym, which flow into Plymouth Sound, one of the finest anchorages in Europe. Plymouth has many associations with the sea; on the Hoe, where Drake is supposed to have played his memorable game of bowls, stands the lighthouse, known as Smeaton's Tower, which stood on Eddystone Rock for 120 years. Plymouth suffered greatly from aerial attack during the last war and the main part of the town has been largely rebuilt.

81

Mullion Harbour (82) is one of the romantic spots of the Lizard Coast.
Le petit port de Mullion (82) est un lieu romantique de la côte du Lézard.
Der kleine Hafen von Mullion (82) ist ein romantischer Fleck der Lizardküste.

Cornwall

The Royal Duchy of Cornwall, the most westerly of English counties, is one large peninsula, and this fact, and its comparative distance from the more populous parts of the country, have engendered an independence of character which makes the county in many ways 'different' from the rest of the West of England. The interior of Cornwall consists for the most part of moorland, with Bodmin Moor the most well-defined area. The Cornish moors are bleak and sparsely populated, but Nature is here completely unspoiled, and there are many interesting little towns and villages. But it is the coasts which are the real glory of Cornwall. The northern – or more properly the north-western coast – is composed of rugged granite cliffs which in winter face the full fury of the Atlantic, and in the more exposed places bear witness to the forces of Nature with which they have to contend. But Nature has more than one mood, and on calm evenings the most beautiful of sunsets irradiate these same weather-beaten cliffs. The southern coast has earned for itself the title of 'the Cornish Riviera', a title which is not undeserved, for although it may lack the sophistication, the glitter and the casinos of the Mediterranean, it has so much to offer in compensation: the most unspoiled of coastal villages, superb scenery and the simple homely friendliness of hard-working people. From Land's End to the Lizard there unfolds a wonderful succession of coves and bays, each differing in detail from its neighbours, yet forming a natural harmony. Few parts of the British Isles enjoy such an equable climate as Cornwall. Near the coasts frost is a rarity and the winters are exceptionally mild. In summer the weather is warm but not uncomfortably hot, thanks to the moderating influence of the sea. Cornwall abounds in legend and romance. The story of the founding of St Ives is typical of the legends which have a religious origin; others are connected with chivalry, especially those concerning the deeds of King Arthur, while some, such as that of the drowned city of Lyonnesse, are legends of the sea.

Until 1832 the twin resorts of East and West Looe were separate boroughs; each had its own coat-of-arms and each returned two Members of Parliament. Today the two towns are administratively united. They lie on either side of a narrow river which forms one of the busiest fishing ports in Cornwall. East and West Looe are joined by a stone bridge of seven arches (83). Polperro (84) was once renowned as a centre of smuggling, but today the little village is an artists' paradise. Its principal attractions are the 'House on the Props', built over the river and supported on stilts, and the 'House of Shells'. Bodinnick (85) lies on the left bank of the estuary of the Fowey, which extends as far as Lostwithiel. The village slopes steeply to the river, which is crossed by a ferry to Fowey. It is no exaggeration to say that Fowey (86) belongs to the sea, for the harbour reaches right up to the houses by the water. It has always been a port, and in the Middle Ages Crusaders set sail from its harbour. From Prussia Cove in the vicinity a notorious smuggler, John Carter, conducted his nefarious enterprises, which earned him the nickname of 'The King of Prussia'. Polkerris (87), on the eastern side of St Austell Bay, was formerly a fishing port, and a stone pier still shelters the beach, which is one of the most attractive on this part of the coast. Porthpean (88), on the other side of the bay, now forms part of St Austell, which is the centre of the china-clay industry. China clay was first discovered in Cornwall in 1755 and the fine quality of the deposits brought considerable prosperity to the region.

83

84

85

86
87

Ce pont de pierre de 7 arches (83) joint les stations jumelles d'East et West Looe. Polperro (84) est un vrai paradis pour les artistes avec la « House on the Props », construite sur pilotis, et la « House of Shells ». Bodinnick (85), sur la rive gauche de l'estuaire du Fowey. Fowey (86) dont le port touche les maisons, a été au Moyen Age le point de départ des Croisés La plage de Polkerris (87), protégée par une jetée de pierre, est l'une des plus charmantes de cette partie de la côte. Porthpean (88) fait partie de St Austell, grand centre du kaolin, qui fut découvert en Cornwall en 1755 et dont les gisements sont de bonne qualité.

Bis 1832 waren East und West Looe eigenständige Marktflecken. Nach dem Zusammenschluß entwickelten sie sich zu einem der geschäftigsten Fischerhäfen Cornwalls. East und West Looe sind durch eine siebenbogige Steinbrücke (83) miteinander verbunden. Polperro (84) ist ein kleines Künstlerparadies. Das Haus auf Pfosten über dem Fluß ist eine Seltenheit. Bodinnick (85) liegt am Ufer der Fowey. Die Stadt Fowey (86) war im Mittelalter Ausgangspunkt für die Kreuzfahrer. Polkerris (87) auf der Ostseite der St Austellbucht war früher eine reines Fischerdorf. Porthpean (88) ist heute ein Ortsteil von St Austell.

88

89

Mevagissey (89) perches on the steep slopes which look down on its harbour, which in the eighteenth century was actively engaged in the pilchard trade, great quantities of the fish being exported to places as far away as the West Indies. The first pilchard canning factory in Cornwall was established here. Mevagissey's double harbour is always a source of interest to the visitor. The two stone piers which protect the inner basin as well as those of the outer harbour are popular as promenades and are particularly favoured by anglers. St Peter's, the parish church, has been considerably restored, but parts of the original Norman building remain, and it is practically certain that a Saxon church once stood on the same site. A few miles to the south-west of Mevaggisey is St Goran – or Gorwean – with a fine church which has a tall fifteenth-century tower. A mile further on lies Gorran Haven (90), which has developed from a fishing village into a popular holiday resort. Two miles to the south stands the mighty headland of Dodman Point, the most prominent coastal feature between Plymouth and Falmouth and now belonging to the National Trust. From the top there are some of the finest views in South Cornwall. Between Dodman Point and Nare Head is the majestic sweep of Veryan Bay. Porthluney Cove, one of the best bathing beaches in the area, lies almost at the centre of the bay. Overlooking the beach is Caerhays Castle (91), which was built by Nash at the beginning of the nineteenth century and which replaces a much older building. Just inland is St Michael's Church, a Norman foundation containing helmets of former warriors. Continuing round Veryan Bay we come to Portloe (92), a quaint old fishing village huddled at the end of a steep valley through which a stream flows into the sea. In some ways the village is reminiscent of Boscastle on the northern Cornish coast. Two miles to the west is Veryan, a village noted for its thatched 'round houses', each of which has a cross at the apex of the roof. According to local legend they were intended to keep the Devil away from the inhabitants.

C'est à Mevagissey (89) que fut établie la première conserverie de sardines de Cornwall; les jetées protégeant les deux bassins du port constituent d'agréables promenades; l'église St Pierre a été considérablement restaurée mais une partie de l'ancien édifice normand est resté. Gorran Haven (90) est devenu un populaire centre de villégiature. Dominant la belle plage de Porthluney Cove, le château de Caerhays (91) a été construit par Nash au début du 19e siècle. Portloe (92) est un vieux village de pêche, blotti au fond d'une vallée escarpée, qui rappelle le village de Boscastle sur la côte nord.

Mevagissey (89) war im vorigen Jahrhundert ein bedeutender Hafen im Sardinenhandel. Hier wurde die erste Sardinen-konservenfabrik Cornwalls gebaut. Die St Peterskirche geht bis in sächsische und normannische Zeiten zurück. Der beliebte Ferienort Gorran Haven (90) entwickelte sich aus einem Fischerdorf. Einer der besten Aussichtspunkte Südcornwalls ist Dodman Point, zwei Meilen südlich von Gorran Haven. Caerhays Castle (91), in der Bucht von Porthluney, steht majestätisch oberhalb des Strandes. Folgen wir der Bucht von Veryan weiter, so kommen wir nach Portloe (92).

90

91

92

93

94

St Mawes (93) et son château du 16e siècle. A Truro (94), le clocher central et la flèche de 240 pieds de haut de la cathédrale sont dédiés à la mémoire de la reine Victoria. Fondé par des colons hollandais, Flushing (95) fut autrefois un port plus important que Falmouth qui a deux fronts de mer, l'un sur la Manche l'autre sur l'estuaire du Fal. Il y a plusieurs bonnes plages, Gyllingvase, Swanpool et Maen Porth (96), où l'érosion a creusé des grottes et des arches dans les falaises. Le port de Falmouth (97) a un profond bassin. Niché dans une crique solitaire du Helford River, Helford (98) est connu pour ses cottages couverts de roses.

Das Schloß in St Mawes (93) war ein Glied in der Befestigungskette für den Hafen von Falmouth. Truros (94) Geschichte geht mehr als 900 Jahre zurück. Flushing (95) wurde von niederländischen Siedlern gegründet. Falmouth ist der größte Stadt Cornwalls. Es herrscht hier ein solch begünstigtes Klima, daß selbst tropische Pflanzen gedeihen können. Es gibt mehrere schöne Strände in der Nähe, darunter sind Swanpool und Maen Porth (96) besonders zu erwähnen. Der Hafen von Falmouth (97) wurde durch Sir Walter Raleigh erstmalig berühmt. Helford (98) ist bekannt für seine mit Rosen bedeckten Cottages.

95

96

97

The beautiful promontory called Roseland lies to the east of the estuary of the River Fal. The only place of any pretensions is St Mawes (93), with a sixteenth-century castle, built as part of the defences of Falmouth Harbour. Truro (94) can trace its history back to pre-Conquest days and was a port long before Falmouth developed. The cathedral, a handsome building in Early English style, was begun in 1880 and consecrated seven years later. The central tower and spire, which rise to a height of 240 feet, are a memorial to Queen Victoria. The village of Flushing (95) lies on the far side of Falmouth Harbour and is connected to Falmouth by ferry. It was founded by settlers from the Netherlands who named it after the Dutch port, and for some time Flushing was a more important place than Falmouth, now Cornwall's largest town and with such an equable climate that many species of tropical and sub-tropical plants flourish in the open. There are two 'fronts', one overlooking the English Channel and the other the fine estuary of the River Fal. There are several good beaches, among them Gyllingvase and, a little further to the south, Swanpool and Maen Porth (96), where the cliffs have been eroded and caves and arches formed. Falmouth Harbour (97) first came into prominence when Sir Walter Raleigh became interested in the fine deep-water anchorage. Today, although no longer an ocean terminal, Falmouth still has considerable interest in the repair of ships. Nestling among the secluded creeks of the Helford River are charming little villages. Helford itself (98) is well known for its rose-covered cottages.

99

Cadgwith Cove (99), on the eastern flank of Lizard Head, is well known as one of the most attractive of the seaside villages of Cornwall's southern coast, which, although they attract many visitors seeking an unsophisticated holiday, have nevertheless managed to retain their unspoiled character. The cove has twin beaches, separated by a tiny headland called 'The Todden', and there is a sheltered natural pool among the rocks. One of the geological curiosities of the coast here is 'the Devil's Frying Pan', which was caused when the roof of a cave fell in and the constant scouring action of the sea resulted in the formation of this great pit in the cliffs. Cadgwith lies at the end of a charming little valley and is noted for its crabs and lobsters, which find a ready market in nearby places. The distinction of being the most southerly point in Great Britain belongs to the Lizard, a rugged promontory in a coast which is rich in history and in legend. Fantastic rock formations, many bearing such picturesque names as 'the Devil's Bellows', 'the Manacle Rocks' and 'Asparagus Island', lend an air of mystery to this wild and lovely coast. To the east of Lizard Head lies Housel Bay (100), which has a good bathing beach and is within easy reach of Lizard Town. On the cliff stands the Lizard Lighthouse, whose beam is one of the most powerful in the world. Just to the east of the lighthouse is another great cleft in the cliffs which was formed in an identical manner to the one at Cadgwith. This one is called 'the Lion's Den'. Kynance Cove (101, 102) lies about a mile from the Lizard and can be approached only at low tide through a cleft in the cliffs. The effect of sunlight on the serpentine of the rocks is an experience to remember. This rock is carved into souvenirs by local craftsmen, and has been used for the modern pulpit of fifteenth-century Landewednack Church. The cliffs which back the cove abound with great caves, most of which have been given names such as 'the Kitchen' and 'the Parlour'. The whole of this region has been designated as an 'Area of Outstanding Natural Beauty', and as such enjoys protection.

Cadgwith Cove (99), avec ses plages jumelles et sa piscine naturelle dans les rochers est un des coins les plus attirants de la côte sud de Cornwall. A ne pas manquer la « Poêle du Diable », grotte dont la voûte s'est écroulée sous l'action érosive de mer. Sur le « Promontoire du Lézard », le point le plus au sud de Grande-Bretagne, les rochers prennent des formes fantastiques, le « Soufflet du Diable », les « Rochers des Menottes », « l'île de l'Asperge ». Housel Bay (100) a une belle plage à baignade. Le soleil sur les rochers de serpentine à Kynance Cove (101, 102) est un souvenir inoubliable.

Cadgwith Cove (99), an der Ostseite der Lizardbucht, ist eines jener Seeorte, die ihren eigenen Reiz erhalten haben. Die beiden zusammengehörenden Strände werden durch eine kleine Landzunge, the Todden, voneinandergetrennt. Die Teufelsbratpfanne ist eine Höhle, deren Decke eingestürtzt ist und so das Innere freilegte. Die Krabben und Hummer von Cadgwith sind weit bekannt. Der Lizard bildet die äußerste Südspitze Großbritanniens. Östlich von Lizard Head liegt Housel Bay (100). An den Kliffs steht der Lizardleuchtturm. Nach Kynance Cove (101, 102) kommt man nur bei Ebbe.

100

101

102

103

104

105

Mullion Cove (103), appelé aussi Porthmellin, est la plus grande crique de la côte du Lézard, avec dans les falaises avoisinantes de très belles grottes. Poldhu Cove (104) connut une renommée mondiale le 12 décembre 1901 lorsque Marconi y reçut le premier signal télégraphique à travers l'Atlantique. A Gunwalloe Cove (105), l'église a un magnifique intérieur avec des fonts baptismaux d'époque normande. Le port de Porthleven (106) construit au début du siècle dernier était déjà connu pour ses constructions de schooners dont quelques-uns furent utilisés par le Hudson Bay Company. En 1807, la frégate Anson fit naufrage près du port ce qui incita Trengrouse à perfectionner son système de fusées porte-amarres. Le Mont St Michel (107, 108) haut de 250 pieds, est rejoint à la terre par une digue recouverte par les eaux à marée haute.

Mullion Cove (103) oder Porthmellin, ist die größte Einbuchtung an der Lizardküste. Die Mauern des romantischen Hafens sind solide gebaut, um den Winterstürmen standhalten zu können. Die Insel Mullion wird vom National Trust unterhalten. Poldhu Cove (104) hat 1901 Berühmtheit erlangt, als dort Marconi die ersten drahtlosen Signale aufnahm. Vor der Bucht von Gunwalloe (105) strandete im 18. Jh. ein Schiff und der kostbare Münzenschatz wurde angeschwemmt. Die Kirche hat ein feines Wagenbalkendach und einen normannischen Taufbecken. Der Hafen von Porthleven (106) wurde erst im letzten Jahrhundert gebaut, davor war nur ein Damm vorhanden. Porthleven ist seit vielen Jahrzehnten für seinen Schiffsbau bekannt. Chevy Chase Hall und die Kapelle auf St Michaels Mount (107, 108) können besichtigt werden.

Mullion Cove (103), or to give it its correct name, Porthmellin, is the largest inlet on the Lizard coast. The walls of the romantic little harbour are strongly built, in order to withstand the heavy seas of winter. In the nearby cliffs are several fine caverns. Off-shore is Mullion Island, which, with the cove, is in the care of the National Trust. A mile from Mullion is Poldhu Cove (104), which achieved worldwide fame on 12 December 1901 when Marconi heard on this spot the first wireless signal from the other side of the Atlantic. Beautiful Gunwalloe Cove (105), with its church sheltering in the lee of the cliffs, has a romantic story. A pirate was believed to have buried treasure here, and in the eighteenth century, one, John Knill, obtained permission to search for it. His search proved fruitless, but some years later a vessel carrying coin was wrecked in the cove and much of the treasure washed up. The church is reputed to have been built as a thank-offering by a sailor who escaped from a wrecked ship. The interior is very lovely, with a fine wagon-beam roof and a Norman font. The harbour at Porthleven (106) was built at the beginning of the last century; before that time there was only a stone causeway there. But Porthleven was well known before that for ship-building, especially for schooners, some of which were used by the Hudson Bay Company. In 1807 the frigate *Anson* was wrecked near Porthleven with a tragic loss of life. This sad event inspired Trengrouse to perfect his rocket apparatus for saving lives at sea. Traditionally St Michael's Mount (107, 108), which lies half a mile from the coast near Marazion, is the ancient Island of Ictis. There was a Benedictine chapel founded here in the eleventh century, which became a monastic fortress. The refectory, known as Chevy Chase Hall, and the chapel may be visited. The Mount, which rises to a height of 250 feet, is joined to the mainland by a causeway uncovered only at low tide. In many ways it resembles the much larger Mont St Michel in Normandy, on the other side of the English Channel.

106

107

108

Penzance (109), la ville la plus occidentale à l'Angleterre, à 2H½ par mer et 20 mn par air des îles Scilly, a un climat si doux que de nombreuses variétés de plantes sub-tropicales y poussent sans aucun mal. Newlyn vit presque entièrement de pêche grâce à l'excellence de son port (110), et est célèbre pour son École de peinture qui a des affinités avec les Impressionistes français. Mousehole (111) prononcez « Mowsell », doit sa prospérité à la pêche à la sardine. Land's End (112), masse rocheuse de 60 pieds de haut, le point le plus occidental d'Angleterre, est d'une beauté grandiose.

Penzance (109) ist Englands am weitesten westlich gelegene Stadt. Ihre Lage an der Mounts Bay ist einmalig schön. Die Stadt ist der Zentralort Südwestcornwalls und Marktort für dieses Gebiet. Selbst die Scilly Inseln senden ihre Erzeugnisse dorthin. In dem milden Klima wachsen selbst subtropische Pflanzen, was in den herrlichen Parkanlagen zum Ausdruck kommt. Newlyn ist bekannt für seine Künstler und den Fischfang. Der Hafen (110) ist das Herz dieses Ortes. Mousehole (111) verdankt seinen Wohlstand fast ausschließlich dem Sardinenfang. Land's End (112) ist der äußerste Punkt Englands.

109

110

111

Penzance (109), England's most westerly town, has a magnificent setting overlooking the wide sweep of Mount's Bay. It is an excellent centre for south-west Cornwall and is the chief market for the varied agricultural produce of the region and of the Scilly Isles, which can be reached by boat in two and a half hours, and by air in twenty minutes. The climate of Penzance is so mild that many species of sub-tropical plants thrive in the open and are seen to good advantage in the well-kept public gardens. Newlyn is only a mile from Penzance, to which it is linked by an excellent coastal road. It is, of course, famous for its artists and its fish. Today the brown sails of the old-time fishing craft have all disappeared and have been replaced by motor-propulsion, but fishing is still the chief means of livelihood. The prosperity of the fishing is due in no small measure to the excellence of the harbour (110), which is large enough to shelter the many craft. Newlyn was burned by the Spaniards at the end of the sixteenth century and there are no buildings remaining of earlier date. The town has the distinction of inspiring a school of painting which has affinities with the French Impressionists. Mousehole (111), pronounced 'Mowsell', can be said to belong to the fishermen, for its prosperity is due almost entirely to that most elusive of fish, the pilchard. When pilchard fishing with seine nets was at its peak Mousehole was one of the leading harbours from which the boats sailed, and there is still a small fleet operating today. Mousehole was formerly known as Porth Enys, the 'island port', from St Clement's Isle which guards the entrance to the harbour. Dorothy Pentreath, believed to be the last person to speak the Cornish language, died here in 1777. Land's End (112), a sixty-foot-high rocky mass, covered with turf, is the most westerly point of England and the many visitors to this spot are rewarded by some of the grandest coastal scenery in Cornwall and the spectacle of Atlantic waves breaking on the rocks at the foot of the cliffs which bear such picturesque names as the 'Irish Lady' and the 'Armed Knight'.

113

114

115

L'archipel des Scilly comprend 140 îles dont cinq seulement sont habitées. St Mary est la plus grande et a pour capitale Hugh Town. Typique de ces îles, New Grimsby (113) a une abbaye construite sur le site d'un prieuré bénédictin du 10e siècle. Sennen Cove (114) est une continuelle source d'inspiration pour les artistes. Cape Cornwall (115) un des deux promontoires gardant Porthledden Bay. St Ives, avec son climat sain, ses étendues du sable, le charme désuet de ses ruelles et de ses maisons est un centre de villégiature privilégié de Cornwall; le port (116) est connu pour son activité.

Die Scilly Inseln liegen 28 Meilen vor dem englischen Hauptland. Insgesamt sind 140 Inseln. Die größte der bewohnten fünf ist St Mary. Eine typische Inselsiedlung ist New Grimsby (113) auf Tresco. Sennen Cove (114) ist besonders bei Künstlern beliebt, die reichlich Anregung in der Umgebung finden. Auf Gurnard's Head stand eine der Küstenburgen Cornwalls. Auf Cape Cornwall (115) findet man ein Hünengrab als Zeugen früher Besiedlung. St Ives ist wegen seiner offenen Lage zum Meer, seinem Klima und seiner Badestrände beliebt. Der Hafen (116) ist das geschäftige Herz der Stadt.

The Scilly Isles, identified in Arthurian legend with Lyonnesse, lie about twenty-eight miles from the English mainland. In all, the group comprises some 140 islands of which only five are inhabited. St Mary's is the largest, and Hugh Town the capital. Memorials to shipwrecked mariners are to be found in the churchyard in the Old Town. Typical of the small island settlements is New Grimsby (113) on Tresco, which has a new abbey on the site of a Benedictine priory of the tenth century. Sennen really consists of two villages, Sennen Cove and Sennen, the latter village being known locally as Churchtown. Sennen Cove (114), situated at the southern end of Whitesands Bay and only just over a mile from Land's End, is especially popular with artists, who find a considerable source of inspiration in the village and its surroundings. The 'toe' of Cornwall is a smaller peninsula of the county, and along its four-mile-long landward boundary runs the main railway to Penzance, but its coast is over fifty miles in length. On Gurnard's Head, formerly called Treryn Dinas, there stood one of the most heavily fortified of Cornwall's cliff castles, and there are still some of the remains to be seen to this day. Porthledden Bay is guarded by two headlands, on the northern of which are the ruins of another cliff castle. The southern headland bears the imposing name of Cape Cornwall (115). Whether there was a castle here is not clear, but there is evidence of former occupation in the existence of a stone barrow, a prehistoric burial-ground, on the cliff edge. St Ives is one of the favourite holiday resorts in Cornwall. Its magnificent situation, extensive coastal views, bracing air and wonderful stretches of sand combine to present a strong appeal, and the town, with the old-world charm of its narrow streets and picturesque houses, is an attractive and romantic spot. The harbour (116) is the focal point of the life of St Ives, both for the activity of the many craft and for the beauty of its setting. The parish church is dedicated to St Ia, the saint who, so legend tells us, came to Cornwall from Ireland in a coracle. Standing as it does right on the shore, the church is one of the most prominent landmarks of the town and well repays a visit. St Ives and its immediate neighbourhood can boast of some of the finest beaches in the west.

116

117

118

Le phare de Godrevy (117), vu de la plage de Gwithian. A Portreath (118), entre St Ives et St Agnes, qui avait autrefois des mines d'étain, est aujourd'hui une agréable petite station. Quay Valley (119) conduit à Trevaunance Cove, jolie baie à la belle plage sablonneuse. Perranporth (120) est un lieu de villégiature populaire avec au nord, les restes de la Chapelle St Piran datant du 6e ou 7e siècle. Le port de Newquay, entre deux jetées de pierre et des falaises vertes, est des plus pittoresques; la large baie est constituée de nombreuses petites plages parmi lesquelles Towan Beach (121) est à juste titre particulièrement populaire.

Vom Strand in Gwithian hat man einen guten Blick auf den Godrevy Leuchtturm (117). Portreath (118) liegt zwischen St Ives und St Agnes. St Agnes war einmal ein Zentrum für den Zinnbergbau. Quay Valley (119) verbindet St Agnes mit Trevaunance Cove, einer schönen kleine Bucht. Perranporth (120) ist ein unverdorbenes Seebad, wo man den modernen Sport von Wellenreiten treiben kann. Von Perranporth kann man gut Ausflüge nach Westcornwall machen, z.B. zu den Ruinen des St Pirangebethauses aus dem 6. Jh. Newquay ist nicht „neu", denn sein Hafen wurde 1615 gebaut. Der beliebteste Strand von Newquay ist Towan Beach (121).

119

120

The little resort of Gwithian is situated on the north-eastern side of St Ives Bay. From the beach there is a good view of Godrevy Lighthouse (117) on an island just off the shore. Nearby are traces of an oratory which probably dates from the ninth century. Portreath (118), once called Basset's Cove, lies at the foot of a wooded combe between St Ives and St Agnes. Its little harbour is still used occasionally, but the narrow entrance can only be negotiated in good weather. Between Portreath and Gwithian there is some fine coastal scenery and much of the area is in the care of the National Trust. St Agnes was once a tin-mining centre but today it is an attractive little resort. Some of its streets bear such quaint names as 'Goonlaze', 'Wheal Kitty' and 'Stippy-Stappy'. From the town, Quay Valley (119) leads to Trevaunance Cove, a beautiful coastal inlet with a fine sandy beach. Perranporth (120), between St Agnes Head and Newquay, is a popular holiday resort and it is a good centre for exploring the west of Cornwall. A short distance to the north are the remains of St Piran's Oratory, dating from the sixth or seventh century. The little church lay buried beneath the sand for many years but it is now protected by a concrete shell. Newquay belies its name, for the quay is not new, having been constructed early in the seventeenth century. The harbour, guarded by two stone piers and fringed by green cliffs, is one of the most picturesque in the West Country. Newquay's large eastern bay is divided into a number of smaller beaches, of which Towan Beach (121) is particularly popular.

122

Bedruthan Steps (122), about eight miles north of Newquay, are among the finest detached rocks in England. The most striking of them is known locally as 'Queen Bess'. According to popular legend these great grey rocks were stepping-stones for the giant of that name. When great waves are breaking over the rocks the spectacle is magnificent. In the cliffs are some remarkable caves, which can be visited at low tide; the largest of them, the Great Cavern, is one of the finest in the country. There is a simplicity about Padstow (123) which endears it to those who prefer the quieter type of holiday. It lies secluded on the left bank of the estuary of the River Camel, and gives little indication of having been a borough in Tudor times. Padstow now lives chiefly by fishing but it is becoming known for its excellence as a holiday centre, especially for the yachtsman and the angler. St Petroc's is the parish church. It dates largely from the fifteenth century and has many treasures, including a beautifully carved font. The strange May Day ceremony of the Sailor's Horse, which is still performed, may have had its origin at Padstow, although it is also to be found at Minehead and Dunster. Polzeath (124), which lies on Padstow Bay, has a fine beach and is extremely popular with bathers and surfers. To the north is Pentire Head, now in the care of the National Trust. Huddled at the foot of the Cornish cliffs in a sheltered cove, Port Isaac (125) is one of the quaintest fishing villages in the West. Nowadays Port Isaac is spreading along the higher ground, but down by the harbour it still wears the air of yesteryear. The little harbour, now chiefly devoted to pleasure and fishing boats, had considerable importance in medieval times, especially for the shipping of corn and other produce of the land. South-east of Port Isaac are the remains of Castle Dameliock, also known as Tregeare Rounds. This was the castle referred to in *Morte d'Arthur* as 'Castle Terrible'. Two of the three original circular ramparts are still to be seen. Today the little resort earns its living chiefly from the catching of shellfish and from the ever-increasing holiday trade.

Bedruthan Steps (122) à 8 milles au nord de Newquay, sont de magnifiques rochers parmi lesquels « Queen Bess » est le plus remarquable; le spectacle des vagues se brisant sur ces rochers est grandiose. Dans les falaise, « Great Cavern » est une très belle grotte. Padstow (123) sur la rive gauche du Camel, commence à être connue des navigateurs de plaisance et des pêcheurs à la ligne; son église possède de magnifiques fonts baptismaux. La belle plage de Polzeath (124). Port Isaac (125) et son air d'autrefois, est un des villages les plus originaux de cette région avec au-sud les restes du « Château Terrible » de Dameliock.

Bedruthan Steps (122) sind isoliert im Meer liegende Felsbrocken. In den Kliffs findet man bei Ebbe besuchenswerte Höhlen. Padstow (123) ist eines der ruhigen und einfachen Küstenorte. Man sieht es der Stadt nicht an, daß sie seit Tudor-zeiten ein Marktflecken ist. Noch bestimmt der Fischfang das Leben seiner Bewohner. Der eigentümliche Maifeiertags-brauch des Seemannspferdes mag hier seinen Ursprung haben. Polzeath (124) bietet gute Gelegenheit zum Wellenreiten. Der alte Teil von Port Isaac (125) erinnert an vergangene Zeiten. Südöstlich liegen die Ruinen der Dameliockburg.

123

124

125

126

127

128

Few more romantic spots exist then Tintagel, where history and legend are so completely interwoven that to attempt to separate them is to destroy the romance of the place. On Tintagel Head are the remains of King Arthur's Castle (126), probably originally a Norman fortress, which was first opened to the public in 1872 and is now an Ancient Monument. Considerable excavation has established that there was a monastery on the site prior to the building of the castle. Boscastle Harbour (127), intricate and mysterious, is set among some of the wildest coastal scenery of Cornwall. The harbour is very old and in rough weather is lashed by the waves, a spectacle which is both beautiful and awe inspiring. The village owes its name to Bottreaux Castle, long since disappeared. It lies at the foot of a very steep hill, and in its main street is a row of ancient limewashed cottages, with curious chimney-stacks, which date from the sixteenth century. Bude (128), the largest resort of northern Cornwall, has a good situation on the estuary of the River Strat. There is another waterway here – the Bude and Holsworthy Canal – built early last century, which was once navigable for over thirty miles.

Les ruines du château du roi Arthur (126), sur le cap Tintagel, terre d'histoire et de légende. Le vieux port de Boscastle (127) dans un des sites les plus sauvages de Cornwall, fouetté les jours de tempête par les vagues, offre un spectacle irrésistible. Bude (128), sur l'estuaire du Strat, très bien situé, est la station la plus importante au nord de Cornwall.

Es gibt kaum einen romantischeren Ort als Tintagel, wo Geschichte und Legende miteinander verbunden sind. Auf der Tintagelspitze sind die Überreste des König-Artur-Burg (126), einer normannischen Festung. Boscastle Harbour (127) liegt an einem der wildesten Küstenstreifen Cornwalls. Bude (128) ist der größte Ferienort in Nordcornwall.

© *Copyright 1973 Jarrold & Sons Ltd, Norwich, England 85306 447 4*
Published and printed in Great Britain by Jarrold & Sons Ltd, Norwich, England 273